Ta|

CARING FOR YOUR BUNNY RABBIT

Handbook Guide to Ownership, Care, Grooming & Training.

Keeping Your Pet Happy, Healthy & Safe

═══════════════

A.L.Peries

Do you have a pet bunny rabbit, or are you considering buying one?

Perhaps you wish to know how to raise a happy and healthy bunny?

This book is written specifically for anyone who owns or wants to keep a pet rabbit. It is your initial step towards understanding and caring for your pet.

You must be aware of the responsibilities that come with bunny rabbit care. This book is suitable for adults and kids and contains facts and answers to common questions that bunny parents need to know.

This easy-to-understand book

has cute decorative bunny illustrations and valuable information that you can put into practice straight away.

The data is appropriate for both the USA and the U.K.

We will cover the basics of keeping a bunny rabbit, from whether a rabbit is a suitable pet for you to the equipment needed for your pet rabbit.

Other questions, tips and tricks like what you should feed your bunny to keep it healthy, where you keep them in, bunny body language, what is your rabbit thinking? Joining groups, where to go for advice. What to do if your bunny is poorly and more etc.

I hope this must-read book will help you to enjoy bunny ownership and interaction.

This book's back is helpful checklists, links, and sources to research yourself, discover more, and increase your and the kids' knowledge!

Do you have a pet bunny?

Here's how to care for them and take the best care of your rabbit.

Rabbits are spotless animals, so you don't have to worry about cleaning their cages out often. Just spot-clean it once a week by removing the urine-soaked litter and any poops, and add fresh hay or straw. The pen should also be wiped down with an ammonia-free cleaner each time you clean it out.

You should also check your rabbit's eyes and teeth at least once a week and take their temperature daily with a thermometer. A veterinarian should check them if they get sick, but call the local animal hospital immediately if you see that your rabbit is not breathing. You should also let them listen to soothing music while they're sleeping (*for example, "Broadway on the bunny" on Spotify*).

Rabbits like to spend time with families and do not like being alone all day long. They are generally very good with children, but they should be watched while playing together because of their small size.

Your rabbit will need to be groomed by you at least three times a week because, along with their fur coat, they have very soft fur on the bottoms of their feet which are easily scratched by litter or dirt. Some people choose to have this fur clipped so that it does not get in the way of them running around.

Tying your rabbit up before you leave the house is not recommended because this can cause stress for them, and it's usually best to not put your pet in this situation.

Make sure that your bunny has fresh food and water at all times. You should also buy them plenty of toys to play with, so they do not get bored when you're away.

Because rabbits are very social animals, they require a lot of interaction to be happy and healthy. They generally love to run and wrestle with their owners, but they also love to spend time sitting on your lap and relaxing.

If you have a lot of time and energy, a bunny would be an entertaining addition to your family.

NOTE: For more information on Rabbits, you can visit the House Rabbit Society website.

https://rabbit.org/

Save an animal, give a home to a homeless pet today!

How Do I Find My Perfect Bunny?

―――――

You should look for a healthy rabbit when deciding which rabbit to choose. It is often better to see all the rabbits in any particular litter if you can do so. Each bunny ought to be active and alert. Their fur coat needs to be packed and shiny, and they need to be looking full and well-fed.

The Best Kind of Bunny

Choosing the right kind of rabbit is essential. Unfortunately, small pet stores often sell sick or genetically unhealthy rabbits and can't run away from you when you walk up to them. Usually, the rabbit is tethered to the floor by a chain and can't reach any of it. In addition, the rabbit, which can be more than a year old, is more likely to have been used as a "breeding" animal for many years, which is unsuitable for the rabbit or you.

If you visit a small pet store and see rabbits of this sort, consider going elsewhere. You will probably either have a very unpleasant experience or won't find what you're looking for at all. In addition, a healthy and young rabbit (under six months) will often be more independent than an older rabbit that has had many years of experience.

It would help if you also got a rabbit from someone who has taken care of rabbits for some time. A good breeder will have lots of experience with rabbits and knows how to keep them healthy.

They may be able to recommend a reputable breeder or perhaps give you the name of one in the area where you live.

What Breed Is Best?

Suitable breeds for beginners are often the four significant breeds:

- *Mini Lop*
- *Mini Rex*
- *Dutch*
- *Polish.*

All four small breeds are known to be reasonably quiet and gentle. However, most types of domestic rabbits can be excellent pets.

Are Rabbits' Good Pets?

———

Rabbits are wonderful pets. They are clean, quiet, and can be litter box trained. They have a pleasant temperament, and their intelligence is high. As a result, they need very little care and can be left alone for short periods without being destructive or causing other harm to themselves.

Rabbits breathe differently from cats and dogs. Rabbits do not have a diaphragm, so when they eat, their lungs expand, which forces the carbon dioxide from their stomachs to be exhaled.

Can Rabbits Be Kept As Pets With Other Animals?

Yes. Rabbits can be kept with other animals, but it is usually not recommended. When they are held together, the rabbits may compete for food, water, and territory.

It is best to keep them in separate cages or small runs of wire-lattice fencing. However, if there are no other suitable housing choices available, the rabbits must be confined not to attack each other or another animal.

What are the most common medical problems experienced by rabbit owners?

The two most common health problems seen in rabbits are respiration and diarrhoea.

The respirate is a condition that causes the rabbits to stop breathing. It is often caused by internal parasites, especially internal parasites of the digestive tract.

Diarrhoea is a standard affair in rabbits caused by internal parasites, but usually due to insufficient fibre in their diet. Adult rabbits should have unlimited hay and a constant supply of fresh, green vegetables.

If you do not want to buy fresh greens every day, you can feed them the pre-packaged rabbit food sold in pet stores. Rabbits also enjoy fruits, which should be given to them in small amounts since they are high in sugar.

Good Pets

In recent years rabbits have been used as classroom pets for reading programs around the world. Lending them to schoolchildren has shown that rabbits are good pets, too. They are sociable, pleasant, friendly and family-oriented. Rabbits do not jump on people. Rabbits come when you call them. They don't chew on furniture or try to escape through the windows. And unlike hamsters or gerbils, they do not need the training to learn habits like nocturnal activity cycles or other tricks like "spin the wheel" (a hamster's wheel is likely to be hard plastic; a bunny's wheel is wood).

In addition to being classroom pets, rabbits make popular "service volunteers" for nursing home therapy programs. They help pass the time positively for people who may otherwise spend a lot of time in bed or sometimes in isolation.

HOW DO I TELL IF A rabbit is sick?

Rabbits that are ill will have a decreased appetite and may spend more time sleeping than usual.

https://www.rspca.org.uk/adviceandwelfare/pets/rabbits

Bunny Rabbits Are Good Pets

The short answer is yes, and they prefer a home setting. However, they do need a lot of attention and exercise to thrive in a domestic environment. In addition, they are not lap-friendly pets and require a lot of room to run around.

They have a very high activity level and love to run around in fresh grass or on the ground if their habitat allows it.

They live underground in burrows in their natural state, so they can't be kept as house pets. It is also not very convenient to pet them; bunnies like to be left alone, and they will not want to be picked up unless you get an older one.

Bunnies like to run around and play fetch, so it's best to let them out of their cage or habitat for exercise every day. However, the activity must be supervised because although rabbits are cute and cuddly looking creatures, they can inflict some severe damage if mishandled.

Do Bunny Rabbits Like To Be Held?

It depends on the rabbit. Most bunnies are very playful and love to be held and petted. However, some rabbits naturally become fearful of people and may not like to be handled by a child.

Does My Bunny Rabbit Need A Litter Box?

Same answer as above – yes and no. Rabbits do not need a litter box; they prefer eliminating it in a quiet, confined area like their cage or hutch, like hay or straw (or even shredded paper). However, if you want to provide your rabbit with a litter box, it can be lined with non-clumping cat litter.

Can My Rabbit Go Outside?

Same answer as above (and below) - yes and no. Rabbits are not very adaptable creatures; they are not like dogs or cats that quickly adapt to new surroundings.

They would be more comfortable in an environment they're familiar with, such as their cage, hutch or playpen. Rabbits are also susceptible to loud noises and will hide when you're not there.

Even if you let them out of their cage/hutch, they will need to be confined in their cage, hutch or pen.

Does My Rabbit Need A Companion Animal?

Yes! Rabbits do best when kept with a companion animal of the opposite sex. If you have a male rabbit, it needs a female for companionship and romance – or at least an outlet for his testosterone.

The Pros And Cons Of Owning An Indoor Bunny Rabbit

———

The pros are that they can live up to 12-15 years, are very cute, have very long lives, have many personalities, and have a healthy diet. In addition, you can bond with them by playing with them or talking or singing to them.

The cons are their poop is messy inside the cages, they are responsible for cleaning out their cages regularly.

In addition, there are some health risks with having rabbits as pets because their diet does not have all the nutrients that wild rabbits have.

What Kind Of Food Should My Bunny Rabbit Eat?

Your bunny rabbit needs to eat some vegetables and fruits. It should be around 80% vegetables and 20% fruits. Fresh veggies are good for them, carrots, celery, apples, broccoli, radishes, lettuce, etc. Some flowers are okay.

The rest of the diet is for their pellets. They need to have timothy hay every day too. This will help them get extra fibre in their diet that they wouldn't get if you didn't give it to them.

How Often Should I Change The Water?

You should change your bunny rabbit's water at least twice a day, once in the morning and once at night. You need to make sure that you are using a bowl that they can't knock over or chew on.

The most important thing is to make sure that the bunny rabbit is happy with his surroundings. If your bunny rabbit seems unhappy, try to figure out what he would like changed about his cage.

What Should I Clean Out First?

When cleaning out the cage, start from the top and work your way to the bottom. You should always clean your cages with soap and water or bunny spray.

When cleaning out the cage, it is common to see poops stuck in different places of the rabbit cage. You can use a toothbrush to scrape them out gently.

This is pretty much what you need to know about caring for my pet bunny rabbit.

What Is The Difference Between Indoor And Outdoor Rabbit Rabbits?

Indoor rabbits live primarily indoors, while outdoor rabbits live mostly outdoors.

Tag: bunny rabbit breeders, bunny rabbit price, how can I find a pet bunny rabbit for sale, pet bunny rabbit for sale, where to find pet bunny rabbit for sale.

How Can I Find A Pet Bunny Rabbit For Sale?

Some stores will let you buy them at the store. Thus, they will be relatively cheap. On the other hand, you can still adopt them online. You can also adopt a rabbit from a shelter or rescue group.

Bunny Rabbit Price:

the price of a bunny rabbit depends on the breed and the colour. Their cost is somewhere between $20 and $100.

You can look up local pet stores that have rabbits. You should also look at Boardinghouses, Pet Stores, Pet Shops, Online Stores. You can talk to your neighbours about them too.

When you bring your pet rabbit home, it is essential to make sure they are healthy and safe.

Make sure you ask your veterinarian about any vaccinations your pet might need. You should also make sure that your rabbit is spayed or neutered after six months of age.

Can I Keep A Bunny Rabbit In My Apartment-Flat?

Rabbits live in cabinets outside in the wild, not usually inside our houses with us. This simple fact alone demonstrates why rabbits aren't pets for most people: simply put, they were never meant to live inside your home.

If you want to keep rabbits as pets, the legal requirements are far greater than any other pet you could consider. The law states that rabbits must be housed in a rabbit-proof fence to prevent escape.

In addition, the cage must be clean and comfortable—ideally, no more than a rabbit's "cage" would naturally live outside in the wild. Also, there need to be two separate cages—one for breeding and one for pet rabbits.

If you can't afford or don't want to go to such lengths, it's best to leave the pet rabbit idea behind. Depending on where you live, i.e., which country or state, please check out local rules and regulations.

There are helpful links at the back of this book.

The U.K. Law On Keeping Rabbits In 2021

From the 2011 Annual Act, An Act to make provision about the keeping of rabbits on a farm, on land used for agricultural purposes and on any land in England on which a rabbit is kept for commercial purposes from April 2021.

A new duty has been introduced to enforce the new law. The responsibility is simple:

Anyone who holds a rabbit must ensure it cannot escape or be injured, injured or killed by other animals.

This duty will only apply if the rabbit owner does not have a license to keep rabbits. This is a standard law duty – the responsibility is an essential part of the law and is not imposed by statute. It is enforceable by everybody and does not need to be proven in court.

What is the Rabbit License scheme?

The Rabbit License scheme was introduced in 2005 and followed several incidents over the previous few years where rabbits were kept on land, causing damage to other animals and crops.

What is happening now?

The Duty of Care Order (DOOC) is in draft form and requires DEFRA/Department for Environment before being brought into the statute.

This would ensure that it is legally enforceable and that the protection of the law from abuse from any person keeping rabbits on their land remains unconditional.

The Protection of Animals Act 1911 makes it clear that keeping rabbits on a farm is an offence that carries a maximum fine of Â£500 with a custodial sentence possible. Still, it does not make a distinction between commercial or non-commercial keeping.

How do I apply for a license?

Contact the local authority in the area where you live if you are unsure who this is, visit www.gov.co.uk.

What Are The Licensing Criteria?

To apply for a license, you need to have two years' continuous residence in the U.K. In addition, you need to prove that you have no criminal convictions no animal welfare convictions within the past five years. Residents of Scotland may also apply for a license if they have been residents in Scotland for at least six months.

The law states that there should be at least two acres of land available for your animals, complete with shelter, food and water. The area must be fenced in.

Rabbits must be kept indoors at night. You are also required to put up signs to prevent people from loitering on your land at night, but you must not equip your land with CCTV.

What Needs To Be Done?

Rabbits should have access to a run of 1m x 2m, must be fixed into fencing that is set into the ground and cannot be moved around.

In addition, the rabbit should have access to fresh grass, shelter and water at all times. The rabbit license should only be used to keep one rabbit. If you own more than one rabbit, you will need to apply for a license for each different type of rabbit.

If the rabbit is kept outdoors, the licensee must ensure the length of fencing between the house and outside is two metres or at least five feet long. If you are making additions to your run, then it must be approved by your local authority. The run must be made of robust and secure metal, and you must fix it into the ground.

Where Can I Keep My Rabbit (S)?

If you live in a listed building or a property within a conservation area, you must apply for permission to keep your rabbit. In addition, you need to allow an officer from the local authority access to your property so they can check for any problems such as pests and weeds.

There is new legislation due in 2012 which will relate to rabbits. This will be the first farmers' E-License. Farmers will keep rabbits on their land as long as they have abided by certain conditions outlined in the license. A license was initially given out in April 2012 and will continue to be issued every year, a six-month renewable period for a minimum of two years.

Where Can I Have My Rabbit (S) Kept?

You cannot have your rabbit (s) kept within a listed building unless you have been allowed by your local authority to do so. Therefore, if you wish to keep your rabbit within a listed building, you must apply to your local authority for permission.

How Many Rabbits Can I Keep?

Depending on where you live, i.e., which country or state, you can apply for one license for each type of rabbit. So, for example, if you are looking after two rabbits, they must both be classified as pet rabbits (non-commercial), not farm rabbits (commercial).

However, you can apply for another license or renew the existing license if the breed is different.

Please ensure to check your locality. Legal requirements can change from time to time.

What Is The USA Law On Keeping Rabbits?

USDA regulations state that rabbits can be kept in commercial housing with no more than six, provided they are less than six months old, have not been spayed or neutered, are not pregnant, and are kept in a cage or other appropriate enclosure.

However, if you own more than two rabbits for commercial purposes, you must obtain a USDA license. Rabbits may be sold commercially if their weight is less than 3 pounds (1.4 kilograms) when sold to the new owner.

Companion Animals

Rabbits are very social animals; they often get along well with cats, dogs, ferrets (and others) but will not form an intimate bond with them as they might do with humans. Rabbits can make a magnificent "companion" animal, however. If you decide to have a rabbit as a companion animal, be sure to get two rabbits - one for you and one for your rabbit.

Bunnies love companionship and will pine away, lonely and depressed if left alone too much.

HOW BIG WILL MY RABBIT Get?

Most rabbits can grow to about 4.5- 8.5 pounds, although males tend to be larger than females (because they have more testosterone or "male" hormones). A small or young rabbit probably wouldn't survive on his own outdoors and therefore needs a companion animal.

Does My Rabbit Need To Be Spayed/Neutered?

Rabbits can reproduce until they are four years old. Spaying or neutering your rabbit allows the female rabbit to go into estrus and be ready for breeding and protecting her offspring and keeps the male from copulating with your child's pet cat.

Spaying or neutering can be done at about eight weeks, the age at which they are most comfortable handling.

Naming Your Bunny Rabbit

——

Common Names:

Bunny, Fluffy, Bunbun or just plain rabbit.

For more names, check out this site:

https://rabbitpedia.com/rabbit-names/

A lot of people do not know the difference between a rabbit and a hare. Rabbits are smaller in size than hares. Wild rabbits are found in most parts of the world in diverse habitats.

They are also kept in captivity in homes as pets in many countries throughout the world.

The main thing that needs to be taken care of is the health of your rabbit.

To take good care of your pet rabbit, you need to be aware of the environment you need to maintain.

Some Of The Most Common Diseases That Rabbits Suffer From Are:

Upper respiratory tract infections, caused by bacteria, viruses and mycoplasma. This is very common in rabbits under six months old due to their low immune system.

The symptoms include a runny nose, a mucus discharge from the nose or eyes and sneezing. It is easily treatable with antibiotics.

Respiratory diseases, such as pneumonia and abscesses in the lung. Sources of this disease are drafts, bacteria and viruses, which can be prevented by regular vet visits, a good diet, and regular doses of antibiotics.

Rabbits eat their faeces to obtain nutrients from their diet that is lost during digestion. This is normal for rabbits but should be done in moderation.

Rabbits should also never be given lettuce or other human foods to eat because they do not have the proper digestive system for it.

Hairballs, a common problem in rabbits

To prevent this, a diet of hay and grass should be given to your bunny daily. Also, a rabbit should be allowed to chew or eat wood products such as carrot sticks or twigs to keep the hair in the digestive tract from growing too large and causing blockages.

Rabbits can also suffer from skin problems such as abscesses and lice.

The type of litter box that your rabbit should use depends on its size and urine number. Each litter box should be cleaned daily. If a rabbit frequently urinates outside the litter box, then a litter trained bunny is needed.

This can be done by keeping a towel over the litter box and allowing the bunny to only go in it. If you want to ensure that your rabbit does not urinate outside of its litter box, you can put a tight-fitting, wide opening over it to prevent them from going out of its litter box.

What Are The Different Species Of Bunny Rabbits?

There are many species of wild bunny rabbits. You can find out more here:

https://en.wikipedia.org/wiki/Rabbit

What Does A Baby Rabbit Look Like?

The baby rabbit is called a kit. A baby bunny can have its eyes open at birth. The bunny's eyes will be closed when the animal is firstborn but will open shortly after birth. A baby bunny will open its eyes within hours after it is born. A newborn kit may weigh between .16 to .22 ounces at birth. Within the first few days, the bunny's eyes will open, and its ears become erect. A baby bunny can have fur or have no coat.

How Long Do Rabbits Live?

The average life span of a domestic rabbit is 8 to 10 years. However, some domesticated rabbits have lived to be 15 years old. The average life span of a wild rabbit is 13 months.

The American Rabbit Breeders Association (ARBA) states that over 30 million rabbits are kept as pets in the United States. The average life span of a European wild rabbit is 12 months.

How Many Litter Boxes Should I Have?

There are two litter boxes per cage. The litter box should be cleaned out at least once a week (more often if you monitor your pet). Do this by removing the used litter and placing it in the trash.

When the cages are first purchased, provide one litter box to each bunny, then after that, use one outside of each cage for the other. Otherwise, use two boxes per cage.

If you are using multiple enclosures in an area with dogs, consider having separate boxes for each rabbit (not recommended).

Can I Keep My Bunny In A Cage With Dogs Or Other Animals?

If you want to keep your bunny in the same enclosure as dogs or cats, make sure that they are separated by something like a screen.

A wire cage will not be able to withstand proper sanitation. Instead, the cage floor should be lined with an absorbent material, such as cedar shavings, shredded paper or hay.

Rabbits love to dig and hide. Rabbits hide in their litter box at night and when they feel concerned. If your bunny is out of his cage, it may be because he feels threatened by your other pets, so try putting the kit back in his cage.

If you are keeping your rabbit outdoors, it should be fenced off not to escape.

How Much Room Do I Need For A Rabbit?

The minimum standard for space for one rabbit is 7′ x 2′ x 2′. The bigger, the better.

How Often Should I Feed My Rabbit?

The correct frequency of feeding is based on the weight of the rabbit. An excellent general guideline is to feed your bunny what he needs (not what he wants). This means that some rabbits will need more than others, but overall, you should provide what they need. The feeding chart below gives the suggested amount of food per day for one rabbit, based on its weight. You can adjust these values based on observation and your pet's condition.

What Is The History Of Pet Bunny Rabbits?

The history of pet bunny rabbits started in ancient Egypt around 3500 B.C. The wild rabbit was domesticated for pet purposes and as a food source because rabbit meat is delicious.

How Much Do Pet Bunny Rabbits' Cost?

It depends on the breed you want to buy because there are different varieties, and each will have a different price. But it ranges from $20 for a simple breed to $500 for the most high-end species such as Holland Lops and Britannia Petites.

What Are The Rewards Of Being A Pet Bunny Rabbit Owner?

The benefits are that you have your living pet bunny to take care of, play with, teach tricks to, and bring happiness into your life. It also helps that pets help lower blood pressure which can help you live a longer, healthier life. The best part is giving your pet the love it deserves, which provides it with purpose in life.

Will My Pet Bunny Rabbit Bite?

There is no such thing as a "perfect pet". Every person and every pet come with their personality, and you must be prepared for a little of everything. Neglecting your pet bunny will only cause them to become aggressive towards you, or worse yet, bite. But there are ways to make your pet bunny feel safe around you without scaring them.

How many exercises Do Pet Bunny Rabbits Need?

You will need to consult with your vet for this question, but generally, rabbits need up to 3 hours of exercise per day. If they don't get enough, not only will they develop health problems, but their metabolism slows down too much for them to gain weight properly.

How Often Should I Bathe My Pet Bunny Rabbit?

When it comes to bathing, you have to pick your poison. Do you want soapy water, or do you want to stick to all-natural products? You should probably stick to all-natural products since soap can dry out their skin.

So, every week your bunny goes without a bath; the first thing that needs to be done is a bath. Afterwards, sudsy water may be used because it is good for the fur/coat of the pet rabbit.

Is There A Way To Make My Pet Bunny Rabbit Less Aggressive?

Yes, you can train your pet bunny rabbit to be less aggressive by following these steps:

First, you must find out why your pet bunny rabbit acts this way and then deal with it. This could be anything from a too-small cage to another animal in the household that they do not like.

Second, you will need to train your pet bunny rabbit to stop biting and use his paws instead. This can be done by using your finger to make the bunny feel comfortable while giving praise like "good boy" and "good girl." You can also use a fake plant or toy to get his attention.

Third, you will need to teach your pet bunny rabbit that the environment should be safe for them. This means that all items in the environment should be out of reach, but if they want something, you must move it so they cannot reach it.

Is It Okay To Leave My Pet Bunny Rabbit Alone For A Day Or Two At A Time?

The first thing you need to ask yourself is: Is it safe for me to leave my pet bunny rabbit alone? If the answer is no, then do not leave your bunny alone. On the other hand, if the answer is yes, then there are a few things that you should keep in mind.

First, you must have a bunny-proofed house so that your pet bunny rabbit cannot get into trouble while you are gone.

This will mean getting a bunny-safe litter box or a way to block up the hole in which they usually go to the bathroom. You can also just keep your home open so that there is no way for your pet bunny rabbit to get into trouble while you are gone.

Second, you must have a friend or family member take care of your pet bunny rabbit during this time.

Third, you must make sure that your pet bunny rabbit is mentally prepared for you to go away. This means that they should be left alone every time you leave the house until you come back.

You can do this by leaving a treat or toy to play with and then putting him in his cage for a few hours. For example, put him in there for 30 minutes on the first day and then leave him alone for a more extensive period. After a few days, they should know that you will always come back.

What Is The Difference Between A Holland Lop And A New Zealand Cross?

The Holland Lop was first bred in the Netherlands, and it has always been a very popular pet rabbit due to its small size and beautiful wool. The New Zealand cross was first bred in the 1950s; to combine the characteristics of a Netherland Dwarf with those of a British rabbit.

It then got its name from the country that was responsible for creating this breed.

Both types of rabbits have the same kind of wool and ears, but even though they were both created to be the smallest breed of rabbit possible, they differ by about ten pounds.

What Can You Do If Your Pet Bunny Rabbit Is Pregnant?

There are many different things that you can do with a pregnant pet bunny rabbit, such as:

Make sure that she has plenty of nesting space. You should also provide her with enough forage and hay. Finally, make sure that she has plenty of water at all times.

Clean out her cage regularly. This will keep everything sanitary, and it will also keep her from being exposed to any illnesses.

Keep an eye on your pet bunny rabbit's behaviour during this time. If you are worried that she may have any kind of problems, then you may have to take her to the vet for a checkup.

What Are The Indoor Bunny Rabbit Breeds?

The best breeds are the Algerian, the California white, the lion head, and blue-eyed rabbits.

What Does The Algerian Breed Look Like?

The Algerian is very small and wiry and is white with black ears, nose, and feet.

What Is The California Rabbit Breed?

The California rabbit breed is white and of average size. It has pink eyes and ears.

What Is A Lion Head Bunny Rabbit?

The lion head bunny rabbit has a fluffy hairstyle and is white with big brown eyes.

What Does A Blue-Eyed Bunny Rabbit Look Like?

The blue-eyed bunny rabbit is small and has long ears, and is white with yellow eyes.

Feeding Your Bunny Rabbit

———

What Foods Should I Feed My Rabbit?

Now that you know how to take care of your bunny inside their cage, it's time to teach them how to feed themselves.

Rabbits are herbivores, which means they need to ingest vegetables and fruit.

Stick to fresh fruits and vegetables, don't give it anything that has chunks or is salty. This will cause your rabbit to get sick very quickly.

You should cut up the food for your pet bunny into small pieces so that they can eat it faster. You can also give them fresh carrots or sweet potatoes because these are good for their teeth and gums.

Giving your fresh rabbit greens like romaine lettuce, spinach or parsley will also help keep their teeth clean.

If you want to make sure that your rabbit doesn't get sick, you should only feed them dry foods (*no wet food*), which are very low-calorie and provide many nutrients for them.

If you can't find rabbit food with low calories, go to the vets and ask what they recommend your bunny eats.

The amount of food they should have per day is around 1/8 pound per day. They will eat as much as they need for the day, so don't worry that they'll overeat or become obese.

In Summary, What To Feed For A Healthy Bunny

- Hay:

Hay is naturally high in fibre and low in fat, making it an ideal bedding material for an animal who will spend most of his life inside his cage. Not only does it help to keep everything clean, but hay is also the primary ingredient in your bunny's diet. Because he cannot digest grass, hay must make up at least 80 per cent of your rabbit's diet. In addition, like humans, rabbits have a high calcium requirement, so feeding a diet that includes a large percentage of hay will help them maintain a healthy bone structure.

- Pellets:

Besides being a great source of fibre, wheat and alfalfa pellets have been fortified with vitamins and minerals. So as long as you provide your rabbit with a variety of types of hay and an adequate supply of pellets, there's no need for your pet to nibble on grass or other vegetation.

- Vegetables:

Rabbit experts agree that you should keep vegetables to a minimum, but they can be a healthy part of your bunny's diet. Since the vegetable matter will have a more challenging time passing through the digestive tract, it adds bulk and helps prevent obesity.

- Fruit:

No fruit should be given to your rabbit without first being cooked. Cooked fruit may also be suitable for rabbits who are overweight or have health problems.

Is There Anything I Should Do To Help My Rabbit Get Into A Healthy Weight Range?

Although rabbits generally live longer than other household pets, living a long and happy life is just as important as living a long life, so you'll want to make sure your pet stays at a good weight.

Feeding your unlimited rabbit amounts of pellets every day will cause him to become overweight, leading to diabetes and even death. You can avoid this by feeding your rabbit at least twice a day in small amounts with plenty of fresh vegetables in the diet.

Let's go to the bathroom.

Don't forget to clean out your pet bunny's litter box every day. Remove the old litter and replace it with new, preferably pine shavings. Make sure that there is enough room for your pet bunny to do his business.

You should also keep their food and water bowls close to their cage so that they can easily reach them whenever they need them.

If you don't have a lot of space, you can get a hanging water bottle so that your bunny can easily reach it.

Equipment Is Needed For A Pet Rabbit

The necessary equipment for a pet rabbit includes a cage, a water bottle, a food dish, bedding.

Every day, pet rabbits need a fresh, clean water bottle to drink from and a food dish to feed them. Bunnies also need to have bedded in their cages. Pet rabbits typically sleep up to 18 hours a day, and the cage needs to be big enough for them to stay in comfortably.

As pet rabbit owners might know, they also require care every day—they need small amounts of hay or straw and regular exercise.

How To Care For Your Pet Bunny Rabbit?

———

A Place For Bunny:

(1) Where To Put The Bunny Cage?

It will be a bad idea if the bunny cage is put next to the fish tank. If you do so because bunny

loves to eat vegetables and also fish as its favourite food. If you do not want your fish to be consumed by the bunny, you should place it far from the fish tank.

If you want to know what the bunny likes to eat what kinds of food, please see the table below.

It will be a good idea if you put rabbit cage at a near distance from the T.V. Because bunny loves to watch T.V., it will feel more comfortable watching T.V. at a close distance from their favourite T.V. program.

(2) How To Clean The Cage?

You should clean the bunny's cage once a week by using dust brushes, later rinse it with water and dry it well.

(3) How To Change The Bed?

Changing the bed varies from 2-3 days for young rabbits, 3-5 days for long-haired rabbits and 5-8 days for woollies. You should also ensure that the bunny cage is always clean and dust-free.

Some rabbits need extra care because they are long-haired or giant breeds.

It would help clean their cage once a week with water and later dry it well at room temperature.

(4) How To Feed The Bunny?

Bunny rabbits' favourite food is carrot because it likes to nibble. So, you should buy some carrots for the bunny. If you want to make sure that your bunny will be dependent on carrots, feed them with young carrots until they are grown up (3-5 months) because they won't like their bowl filled with vegetables.

Rabbits also like hay and grass. So, you can give them grass or hay with seeds or corn as a supplement. The water should be changed once or twice a week.

(5) Which Type Of Bedding To Use?

You can use both blankets and hay for the rabbit cage bedding. But please remember that your bunny needs clean and dust-free. We recommend using Rabbit Cottage Hay Bedding because it is high-quality natural bedding that does not affect the rabbits' health, but it is also low in dust and has good absorbency.

(6) How To Toilet Train The Bunny?

Very easy, just place the bunny at a place you want, then the bunny will know where to toilet.

Please remember that bunny rabbits are susceptible to their surrounding environment. Because they are small animals, so they are quickly being bullied by cats or dogs. That is why it is better to keep your rabbit in a safe cage away from the other pets in your house.

The ideal situation for bunnies is having an outdoor hutch with an attached run. Be sure the cat cannot have access to it.

Carrying a bunny is not a good idea since it can hurt its spine, so you should only keep your bunny as a pet.

How To Bunny-Proof Your House

―――

Bunny-proofing your home is the first step in caring for your pet rabbit.

Rabbits can be destructive and chew on anything they find, so you'll need to keep them out of as many rooms as possible.

You should also avoid giving them anything safe, such as plastic or any non-organic materials.

Caring For Your Bunny Rabbit

What Else Do I Need To Know About Taking Care Of My Bunny?

- Rabbits are social creatures, so they should be kept in pairs or groups. If they live alone, they will suffer from loneliness, which will cause depression, and they will stop being so social. So, if you have one rabbit, it's best to get two.

- Rabbits are naturally clean animals, but they will get dirty when you clean their cage. So, make sure to keep their cage neat and clean so that your pet bunny feels comfortable.

- When you first bring your new pet rabbit home, it can be a little overwhelming for them, so make sure to spend time with them every day for at least 15 minutes. They will get used to you and feel safe around you in a short time.

- You should not give your rabbit any dog food. Dogs are carnivores, and rabbits are herbivores. Your pet rabbit should be fed fruit and vegetables only.

- When you're cleaning out their litter box, make sure that you throw away the waste in their litter box, but don't flush it down the toilet.

- The vet will help you with other information about taking care of your pet bunny, like how to take care of their teeth and gums. If you do not follow the above care sheet, your bunny will get sick very quickly.

Also, make sure to always check your rabbit's ears and eyes for any signs of infection before going to the vet.

How Do I Clean And Care For My Pet Rabbit's Ears?

When bathing your rabbit, use a damp cotton ball or cotton swab to clean his ears. Make sure you don't use human shampoo, as it will dry out the skin and cause problems with his feet and ears. You should also avoid using wool swabs as these can irritate your pet's sensitive skin.

How Do I Take Care Of My Pet Bunny's Eyes?

If you want to prevent your bunny from having an eye infection or accidentally scratching them, then it's best to wash them regularly with warm water and mild soap. You can use a dropper to soak his eyes in bad eye drops. Just be sure not to use human shampoo because this may dry out his skin and cause problems with his feet and his eyes. The human shampoo also causes burns to the rabbit's footpad.

Training Your Rabbit

One of the exciting things about rabbits is that they can be easily trained to use a litter box. But, like all pets, they crave to have a familiar smell in their litter box because humans' scent is one of the most typical smells for rabbits.

By using litter cake (*a mixture of litter and newspaper*), you can train your bunny to use the litter box efficiently because they like to eat anything in the litter box.

The best time when training your bunny is when it is about six months old because they are most susceptible to new ideas.

Rabbits are intelligent, curious and friendly creatures. Rabbits learn quickly and love to be taught, so reading a rabbit book or watching a video on training your rabbit may be helpful.

If you have never trained a rabbit before, it might be best to consult an expert first.

How Do I Know If My Rabbit Is Happy?

Rabbits communicate with each other by thumping their hind feet, so if you hear a rabbit tapping his back feet – it means he's happy – and you should, too. Rabbits also show affection through nudging and nipping. Your bunny will also vocalize when pleased – a soft "grunt" or purr.

How Long Do Rabbits Live?

Rabbits can live 6-10 years or longer with proper care. People often underestimate the importance of spaying and neutering your rabbit; this is very important in extending your rabbit's life.

A rabbit's diet can also affect his life span; they can quickly become overweight, shortening their lives. Adult rabbits should be fed about 1/4 cup of high-quality pellets per 5 pounds of body weight daily in addition to unlimited hay.

What Are The Most Common Rabbit Diseases?

Rabbit Health News is not a veterinary publication. Please contact your local veterinarian when in doubt.

A rabbit is more likely to become ill if its diet is not balanced or overweight.

To protect your rabbit from illness, make sure they drink plenty of fresh water and exercise regularly.

Bunny Maintenance

———

You should make the litter box more attractive to the rabbit by adding a short length of a perfume bottle. However, make sure you don't put too much scent. Otherwise, your rabbit may become ill.

You should also ensure that your bunny always has free access to water and eat food pellets because this will help them develop their "stomach" and digest their food.

A rabbit's faeces should be changed once or twice a day.

Rabbits can be left out for short periods but should always be kept indoors at night. Please keep them in a safe place away from chicken coops or other areas where other pets may harm them during this time.

You should also provide your rabbit with plenty of room to move around in, which is especially important if it has not yet developed any "long" fur. This will help it become more agile and less prone to injury.

To keep your rabbit's fur clean, you should use a hutch with wire floors. The wire floor prevents your rabbit from burrowing and allows it to stretch out its legs for exercise.

If you don't have the space for a hutch, there are other alternatives, such as moving the rabbit cage to a larger area or placing it in an open room (if this is not possible). Remember to keep the temperature of the room (*and your bunny*) at an acceptable level.

Although rabbits can tolerate colder temperatures, they must be kept at a level where they do not suffer from this. This way, you can ensure that your rabbit remains in good health and that its fur looks excellent!

You should also keep your bunny away from direct sunlight since it might get sunburn.

Litter Train Your Bunny In 8 Steps!

D oes it have to be a litter tray? I'm just wondering because my bunny is about a year old. He has been trained to use a litter box now, but the only thing I have now is a litter tray. He doesn't go in it, though. Instead, he likes to go in his "nest".

Well, first, you need a cage big enough for the rabbit to move around and so he can't injure himself or other rabbits or people.

Second, you need to find a way to keep him in the cage. Bunnies are slippery little guys. Usually, I put my bunny in his cage with food and water. Then, I tape the door shut so he can't get out of his cage. Many people have accomplished this by taping the side of the cage to the table, so they can't jump out even if they try!

Third, you need some sort of bedding for your bunny. It can be a small litter box, a giant litter box, a cat litter box, a child's sandbox, etc. Whatever it is, make sure that your bunny can fit into it comfortably and that he doesn't have too much space. One of the most common mistakes is to give him too much space. I've seen some bunnies with whole bedrooms as their "boxes".

Fourth, you need to teach him how to use the box. Remember that bunnies are very smart and have pretty good memories. Get yourself some hay. Put some hay in the box, too. Put your bunny in the box, along with a small treat. I give my bunny a piece of fruit or an organic strawberry. It's healthy for him and makes him want to pee or poop, which is what you want at this point! Soon enough, your rabbit will use his box as his bathroom!

Fifth, you need to make sure your bunny is comfortable with his new setting. If you're putting him into his cage with food and water, then just leave him. If you're putting your bunny into his box, then just leave him there for a few hours, giving him some hay if he needs it. Your rabbit will probably be scared at first. He's used to the outdoors, and now he's stuck in this weird box with wires or toys around him. He doesn't know what to do! Just leave him alone for a while so he can adjust.

Don't expect him to eat his food right away. It will probably take a few days before he realizes that you put him in the cage/box to be left alone, not for punishment.

Sixth, you need to check on your bunny every so often. Make sure everything is fine and that he isn't stuck or hurt. It's okay to go in and check from time to time.

Seventh, you need to stop feeding him treats and start giving him veggies and fruits instead. I would give my bunny a whole strawberry or an apple, but he doesn't like it. It's pretty easy to wean your bunny off treats or cheap hamburgers and stuff like that.

Eighth, you need to start cleaning the box sometimes, maybe every other day. It's straightforward to do. Just take the old litter box out and put a new one in. It takes like five minutes.

And that's it! You're done litter box training your pet bunny! I hope this helped!

Ten Top Tips Keeping Rabbits

———

(1) Bunny should not be kept with other pets such as cats and dogs because they might get bullied by their cat friend.

(2) Rabbit's cage should be kept at a distance from the fish tank.

(3) It is not a good idea if you clean your rabbit's cage with water and then dry it at room temperature. Because this will decrease its fur lustre, and it might get an illness.

(4) You should not wash your rabbit's cage with water and then dry it in the sunshine because this will remove its fur lustre.

(5) You should not clean your rabbit's cage with water and then dry it at room temperature because this will decrease its fur lustre.

(6) You should not wash your rabbit's cage with water and then dry it in the sunshine because this will remove its fur lustre.

(7) You should not wash your rabbit's cage with water and then dry it at room temperature because this will decrease its fur lustre.

(8) You should not clean your rabbit's cage with water and then dry it in the sunshine because this will remove its fur lustre.

(9) You should not keep a fish tank near a rabbit's cage because the fish smell might bother the bunny.

(10) You should not keep a fish tank near a rabbit's cage because the fish smell might bother the bunny.

If Your Bunny Rabbit Is Unwell

———

How do I know if my rabbit is sick?

Rabbits are very good at hiding their illnesses from you – so the best thing to do is monitor your rabbit's behaviour and watch for any changes in his behaviour or appearance.

Contact your veterinarian if you notice any of the following symptoms:

- *Sudden change in appetite*
- *Sudden change in activity level*
- *Lethargy or decreased interest in play or food*
- *Loss of weight without diet changes, diarrhoea, constipation, bloat, etc.*
- *Difficulty breathing, open-mouth breathing, wheezing/ coughing, sneezing/snuffling noises that are persistent. Rabbits can be heard wheezing when they first wake up or after exercise.*

If you notice any of these symptoms, contact your veterinarian immediately.

How Do I Tell A Male Rabbit From A Female Rabbit?

Male rabbits have a V-shaped sexual swelling in the prepuce or scrotum, and their penis is usually pink with a large head.

Female rabbits have a small teat at the end of their vulva called a clitoris. The scrotal skin is generally tight, with an indented abdomen in males and females.

What Should I Do If My Rabbit Bites?

There are many things you should do if your rabbit bites you. But, first, what does a rabbit bite feel like? Here is an explanation of what can happen when a rabbit bites. When I was bit by my bunny, I was lucky to have the rabbit's foot against his front teeth, which caused minor damage.

If your rabbit bite leaves minor marks on your skin, please visit your doctor to see what else might be wrong with the animal or take i-Vein to prevent infection and blood loss.

WHAT TO DO IF YOU ARE Bitten?

The first thing (and best) to do in a rabbit bite is applied pressure in the form of a band-aid or gauze pad. If you don't have any available, ask anyone in your family for the materials. Hopefully, they will be able to help you. When my bunny bit me, he (he!) yanked on my top lip. At the time, I was unaware of this fact. It was only when I had to clean up the blood that I discovered this.

Overweight Rabbit

This means your rabbit is overweight. To help your rabbit lose weight, make sure to give him unlimited hay and put all food dishes in the cage/hutch/pen, leaving no high perches for him to jump onto. If you've already done this, try putting a "rabbit porch" outside for him to get some fresh air.

You can also limit his pellets intake to just over 1/4 cup per 5 pounds of body weight daily. If you're not sure about the amount of food he should be getting, consult your veterinarian.

Bunny Rabbits Low Maintenance

They are not, contrary to what many people think.

Taking care of rabbits can be pretty tricky, especially if you have little or no experience with the pets, because they require proper attention and maintenance.

So, let's see now how much time do rabbits take to take care of?

First Things First

When you first get your pet bunny, keep it in a cage until he grows accustomed to it. The cage should have plenty of ventilation and run at least 30 watts.

The cage should also have a water bottle and a food bowl placed at a height that your pet bunny can easily reach.

Aside from this, you should give your rabbit a place to sleep. It's best to make it out of hay, as this is natural for them, and they'll feel more comfortable sleeping on it.

You should change the bedding weekly as the rabbit will most likely use pee as a way to mark its territory.

Do You Have A Litter Box?

You can get one from any pet supply store, but you will need to fill them with litter twice a week.

Bedding for the litter box should be changed twice a month or when it gets dirty. This is to prevent your rabbit from using sand in it as this will block their digestive system and cause the sand to clog up their intestines which can be fatal in some cases.

The cage should have a sturdy bottom that is not easily moved and a higher shelf in the cage that your rabbit can jump on for physical exercise. It should also have plenty of sleeping space for your pet bunny to rest during the day.

Bunny Pedicure

———

R abbit's nails grow continuously and will grow so long that they curl under their feet's if they aren't kept trimmed.

You can keep your rabbit's nails trimmed by filling a small container with thick, waxy candle wax and letting the bunny walk around in it. The wax will harden as it cools, lifting the excess hair away from the nails.

You can then use a pair of pinking shears or dog-grooming clippers to cut the excess nail away, making sure not to cut too close to the skin.

How Do I Trim My Bunny's Nails?

First, sit down on a flat surface and place your bunny on your lap.

You should then gently hold his hind paws up and trim the nail on one paw at a time (*if you do both paws at once and he moves, you'll cut him*).

Use a pair of scissors and cut just below the tip of your pet's nail.

Grooming Your Rabbit

———

Your rabbit has a fantastic coat of fur, which is known as wool. You will need to do three things to keep your rabbit's coat in top condition.

They are:

Brush your rabbit. Your rabbit will have a much healthier coat if it is regularly brushed. If you have a long-haired rabbit, it needs to be brushed daily, or at least every other day.

The type of brush you use for this will depend on the kind of fur your pet has. You can use a rubber grooming mitten or a brush with extra-soft, multi-layered bristles.

Wash your rabbit. Your short-haired rabbit doesn't need to be bathed more than once every week, but your long-haired rabbit will need to be washed regularly. You can use an animal shampoo or baby shampoo, which you can pick up from most pet shops. It will help make your rabbit feel a lot more comfortable and keep the fur nice and clean.

Trim your rabbit's nails. Rabbits have very sharp claws, which can easily damage soft furnishings and furniture. Therefore, regular trimming is essential, especially if your pet lives in a house with pets such as cats or dogs. You can choose from different nail clippers that can be used on both short and long-haired rabbits.

Bunny Playtime

What About Playtime?

To give your pet bunny the energy they need for daily activities, you should let them run around as much as possible. You should also let them jump onto high shelves as this will give them exercise.

Jumping helps to remove any unwanted fluids from their bodies and gives them the strength they need for running around.

When you play with your pet bunny, make sure that there are no wires or objects that they can fall off of. You want to make sure that they don't get hurt during playtime.

You should also let them go outside the cage every day, even if it's for a little bit each day. If you put them outside their cage, make sure they are secured in your arms so that they won't escape or run away.

If you're not able to do this, you can put them in a playpen outside of their cage, but make sure that they are not left for long periods; otherwise, they will get bored and start gnawing at their cages which could cause the wires to break.

When you bring your rabbit back inside the house, clean them by bathing them with a mild shampoo.

After their bath, make sure they are dry before you put them in their cage.

Furry Friends

How Do I Take Care Of My Rabbit's Fur?

Rabbits have short fur, so it doesn't take long for them to get dirty. You need to brush your pet bunny's fur once or twice a week to remove any dead hairs and keep the fuzzy look on their bodies.

If you notice that they have lost hair, you can use a comb to help you remove the loose hair. You can also give them a bath to help you remove the dead hair.

Brushing your pet bunny will help their fur to look healthy and eliminate dirt and loose fur. Make sure that you brush them in the direction they naturally grow their fur in.

Since you're going to brush your pet bunny, you should also trim their nails when they get too long. If your rabbit's nails are too long, then they can hurt themselves. If you don't want to trim them yourself, go to a local vet and ask them to do it for you.

Your pet bunny may hate this when you first start brushing them, but when the pet gets used to it, they will enjoy the time that they spend with you.

Benefits Of Keeping Pet Bunnies

The benefits of keeping pet bunnies are numerous. Many people keep them as pets even though they aren't common house pets. The reason why they are so quiet is that they don't talk much. A bunny doesn't need a lot of space to feel comfortable and wanted when in your home.

Since it doesn't move around much when inside your home, you can place it in a smaller cage and not worry about it getting hurt if you happen to bump into it when walking around accidentally. It doesn't need a lot of space to make matters worse if you happen to bump in it accidentally in the dark with a pair of safety goggles on, you can't see it.

Bunnies make a lovely friend in the house, and if you want to show your love for your bunny, there is a way you can express that love. What better way to show how much you love them than by giving them gifts?

Bunnies are playful creatures, so you have to make sure they have enough toys to play with. Since it is small, you can fit a lot of toys inside their cage.

The playfulness of bunnies is often overlooked, so people think they are boring because they look like stuffed toys. This may be the case, but when you get with a friend or family member who has one, you will eventually see how lively they are.

It is also good to remember when you get a bunny that they are not house pets. They do not need to be out in public with you; inside the house, they belong.

You will want to make sure that your bunny's cage has a source of food and water, even if it is in the same room with them all day long. This will make sure that your pet bunny always has access to food and water.

Join Rabbit Groups: Meet Local Pet Rabbit Owners & Lovers

———

B unny Clubs are a great way to meet other pet rabbit lovers and share ideas and information on caring for your bunny. Please be aware that we list the groups we know about and that if you do not see your particular area listed on our website, we do not know of a Rabbit Club in your area. Contact your local animal shelters, humane societies, pet supply stores and vet's offices for more information on starting a club in your area.

Members of rabbit clubs are also very willing to share their love of rabbit care with you.

Many are happy to answer questions via email or phone, or they can recommend books or websites that you can check out for more details on the subject.

Groups are also a great way to get your bunny spayed or neutered. Many rabbit clubs have funds available to help members with the cost of the surgery for their rabbits.

You can also find local pet rabbit owners through Rabbit Lovers Groups that will always list upcoming events where you can meet people locally.

Some of our favourite clubs are:

- *Alabama*
- *Georgia*

- *Idaho*
- *Indiana*
- *Massachusetts*
- *Michigan*
- *Montana*
- *North Carolina*

Bunny Rabbit Body Language

H ow can I tell what my bunny is thinking? (Rabbit body language)

Bunnies have a language of their own, and it's essential to understand it. For example, learning your bunny's body language can help you understand why he is doing what he is doing and help you better communicate with him.

On the table

Laying on the table is usually a sign that your bunny wants some attention or he's looking for something to chew on. If you see your bunny on the table, pick him up and give him some attention. I've found that most bunnies do enjoy being held in their human's arms. Sometimes when they are on the floor, they may be looking for something to chew on.

So, if you see your bunny on the floor, holding onto his favourite toy will be a good thing (if he can't pull it out of your hand), and if he's looking for something to chew on, try to find him some safe items that are already attached to the floor.

Always listen to your rabbit's body language before punishing him. If you punish him for something that is simply not wrong, he will quickly learn that this behaviour effectively gets what he wants. And then next time, there's no telling what he'll get into trouble for!

Scratching

Rabbits have scent glands on the underside of their front paws, just above the "thumbs". A rabbit will scratch the ground after depositing to leave his mark on his territory. If you notice your bunny scratching more frequently than usual, some possible reasons could be related to territorial issues, or it may be related to some sort of medical problem.

Sleeping

Rabbits are at their most vulnerable when they are asleep. You should never approach any rabbit that is lying on the ground. If you notice that your bunny is sleeping, try not to let ANYONE approach him without your permission. It's essential that your bunny feels safe and secure, so if you're not there, he will need to have a buddy with him.

Making a nest

If your rabbit begins making a nest, it is a sign that something is bothering him. Sometimes, making a nest can be as simple as wanting a softer place to sleep. Other times, the cause may be more serious such as stress from being handled too aggressively or loneliness from being separated from his friend.

Excessive sniffing and chewing

Rabbits have poor eyesight and rely mainly on their sense of smell to find their way around.

If your bunny is constantly sniffing the ground or walls, he might be trying to find a missing rabbit from his group. If your bunny is chewing on something it shouldn't be, let him know by positive reinforcement. Food and toys are the most common things your rabbit loves to chew on, so use those as favourable reinforcement.

A bunny as a person

Rabbits as pets can be more than we can sometimes handle, especially if we don't have proper training or knowledge of managing them.

Rabbits are shy by nature, and they can be very fearful of us. So they'll need time to get used to us, just like we need time to get used to them.

The most common reasons rabbits become aggressive are owners who do not adequately train their rabbits or take time to make their rabbits feel comfortable. A rabbit's feeling of safety is usually violated when he gets scared or his trusted environment is broken (*like when strangers come into his house*).

Most rabbits learn very quickly, especially if they are given attention and treats as a reward. The best method is to use food or toys as rewards. If the rabbit senses that you're trying to help him, he will let you know by showing y you understand him. The best way to do this is to learn the language of his body.

Again, you should never approach any rabbit while sleeping (*unless he constantly contacts you*). If you feel like your rabbit needs some time to relax or recover from his fear, then help him by laying down next to him and letting him know that everything's okay. If you're not there, make sure your rabbit feels safe and secure by having a buddy with him (*and don't forget the bunny-proofing!*).

As you take the time to understand what your rabbit is trying to tell you, he will eventually begin trusting you. If you do not understand him, start learning his little language, and soon he will start asking for more attention.

Sometimes it may be better if the rabbit goes somewhere else, even if it's just for a while. Remember, your bunny's feeling of safety is what will keep him coming back to you.

Bunny Rabbit Checklist

-Clean the cage regularly, at least once a day. It is imperative to clean the cage weekly, at least because it is the primary job of owners to make their pets happy.

-Feeding the bunny rabbit with average sizes of bread. Do not use grass very much because it will cause problems for your rabbits during pregnancy.

-Providing fresh water in the cage at all times. Do not allow stagnant water.

-Provide a hutch nearby hutch or placing a cabinet near the toilet so that the rabbit can quickly go through it without getting bothered by other animals and people outside.

-Provide enough space for sleeping and jumping.

-Never give any kind of drugs to your rabbits because it will cause harm to their health like weight loss, nausea, and vomiting. Instead, you can try this herbal diet for your pet bunny rabbit instead of any other regular available diet.

During winter, keep the cage inside the room to have enough warmth for your pet rabbits.

-Placing some hay or wood chip in the cage to provide a more comfortable sleeping area for them. It is good to use plant-based bedding. However, hay may cause problems in the digestion system for baby rabbits. Also, it is not very good for pregnant rabbits.

-Placing some toys in the cage so that your bunny rabbits can play with them and get more fun and enjoyment.

-Try to purchase a rabbit harness and collar so that you can take your pet for a ride because every pet loves to get attention from his master or owner.

About The Author

—

A.L Peries, aka Anthea Peries BSc (Hons), is a published author; she completed her undergraduate studies in several sciences, including Biology, Brain and Behavior and Child Development.

A graduate member of the British Psychological Society, she has experience in counselling and is a former senior management executive.

Born in London, Anthea enjoys fine cuisine, writing and has travelled the world. She has a spoilt but cute but naughty black and white cat named Giorgio and two fluffy bunnies named Puff and Piff.

Other Books By This Author

Anthea has published books in many different genres. You may be interested in other self-help books by Anthea Peries, particularly about bereavement, funerals, chemotherapy treatment, other areas such as eating disorders, food addiction, binge-eating, sugar cravings, emotional eating, or night eating syndrome, insomnia and much more.

Useful Links & Other Sources

Https://www.gov.uk/licence-wild-animal[1]
https://www.gov.uk/government/publications/
rabbits-on-farm-welfare/caring-for-rabbits

https://www.rspca.org.uk/adviceandwelfare/wildlife/
captivity/licences

https://wabbitwiki.com/wiki/
Rabbit_ownership_laws_in_the_US

https://wabbitwiki.com/wiki/
Getting_started_with_a_rabbit

http://www.wikihow.com/Care-for-My-Pet-Rabbit

https://rabbitpedia.com/rabbit-names/

https://en.wikipedia.org/wiki/Rabbit

https://thebritishrabbitcouncil.org/

https://www.gov.scot/publications/licensing-dog-cat-rabbit-
breeding-activities-scotland-summary/pages/4/

https://www.get-licensed.co.uk/licence/animal-activities-
licence

https://www.nidirect.gov.uk/articles/housing-rabbits

---

1. https://www.gov.uk/licence-wild-animal

https://www.meetup.com/topics/rabbits/

https://www.bva.co.uk/take-action/pet-rabbits-pairs-or-groups/

Additional Websites For Pet Rabbit Care

―――

The **House Rabbit Society** is a non-profit educational organization founded to promote the humane treatment of domestic rabbits.

The House Rabbit Society was founded in 1990 by the late Florida veterinarian Dr Margery Glickman, who taught courses on rabbit behaviour, housing and medical care for ten years at the University of California-Davis School of Veterinary Medicine. Glickman's work was carried on by her colleagues, including veterinarian Dr Julie P. Levy, DVM, who became President of The House Rabbit Society in 2005.

The House Rabbit Society provides extensive information about rabbit care and behaviour. They have a wealth of articles, merchandise and supply referrals. In addition, their website has a beneficial Frequently Asked Questions section with in-depth answers to pet rabbit care questions.

The House Rabbit Society also offers live-action video cameras in the sanctuary to allow people to watch rabbits, but it takes a few weeks to process the tapes.

The Pet Industry Joint Advisory Council (PIJAC) is a member-based organization that works with pet manufacturers, veterinarians and other industry professionals to help ensure safe and effective marketing of pets in pet stores.

In addition, the PIJAC provides information on rabbit nutrition, tropical disease management, anaesthesia, emergency medicine and many other veterinary topics through their website.

Like House Rabbit Society, the PIJAC is a non-profit organization dedicated to improving the welfare of companion and pet rabbits and educating the public about rabbits as house pets. If you live in New Jersey, New York or Connecticut, you may also be interested in visiting their chapter website, where you can learn more about rabbit care or even adopt one of these homeless bunnies.

The Better Business Bureau for Better Business Bureau has a resource section on rabbit care that may also be helpful.

The American Veterinary Medical Association's Pet Care Library is a searchable online database that provides veterinary reference materials for veterinary professionals and pet owners. The AVMA also has information on rabbit care, diseases and vaccinations.

The Rabbit Education Society is a small rescue and education group founded in 1986 in Los Angeles, California. They have only one paid employee but are run by hundreds of volunteers with the mission to "*educate children about animals, encourage them to treat animals with kindness, mercy and respect and keep neglected animals safe.*" By visiting their website, you can find out more about their organization, upcoming events or just look at cool pictures of rabbits.

The **Rabbit Rescue League** is a non-profit organization that rescues and finds homes for rabbits and bunnies in need. They have a website with information on rabbit care, rabbit history, and their website may also include links to other groups and pet rabbit enthusiasts.

Visit their website to learn more about the American Pet Products Association's (APPA) mission and mission statement.

They also have a great information section on rabbits that may answer many of your questions about rabbit care.

Puppy Information

-Bunny Care

-Dog Information-Caring for My Pet Poodle and Dog Information

-Caring for My Pet Cat and Cat Information-Caring for My Pet Guinea Pig and Guinea Pig Information-Caring for My Pet Chinchilla and Chinchilla Information-Caring For My Pet Hamster and Hamster Information

- Caring for My Pets Gerbil and Gerbil Care - C.

New Hampshire

- North Country Rabbit Club of New England

- East Coast Rabbit Club of Northern New England

- Caring for Rabbits in Northern New England

- Central Vermont Rabbit Club

- Carving Out A Home For Bunnies in Vermont and the Northeast

- South Shore Pet Rabbit Club of Massachusetts and New Hampshire's: Small Animal Hospital:

Pet Boutique:

Bunny Biz: Pet Paws: Butch & Butch's.

Also, see the House Rabbit Society's club directory for more listings.

Thank you for your purchase. We hope you found this book valuable. Please give us a thumbs-up if it was useful. Your feedback is most important to us!

I thank you in advance.

Don't miss out!

Visit the website below and you can sign up to receive emails whenever A L Peries publishes a new book. There's no charge and no obligation.

https://books2read.com/r/B-A-HIJQ-DMJSB

BOOKS 2 READ

Connecting independent readers to independent writers.

CPSIA information can be obtained
at www.ICGtesting.com
Printed in the USA
BVHW041623240922
647655BV00007B/33

9 798201 062040